FOREWORD

Like an electrifying aria, Ninel Nekay's sharp poetic scene, "The Shortest Film," gripped me, made my blood tingle, prickled up my skin, and resonated across the chambers of my heart. It is unapologetically raw. *Aria* is the fruit of Ninel's operatic piece that has inspired a collection of scenes. Each piece is self-contained and features the singular voice of the playwright, but like an aria in an opera, they are all moving parts that make up a larger work. When stitched together, these scenes create something whole, something alluring and grand: a theatrical play.

When envisioning *Aria*, I was hungry for more scenes that spoke powerfully through sparse dialogue, through the words kept tucked away by the characters on the page, and through the characters' actions. I also wanted to see the writer experiment on the page with space and form—to deviate from set genres and venture out of their comfort zone. It was a promising concoction for magic on the page. And did that concoction work.

I would like to applaud the playwrights of *Aria*—their creative risks cast spells that brought this vision of a collaborative script to life. Thank you for taking a creative leap and producing thrilling poetry set in the dramatic form. I want to thank all
who had a hand in this production, from layout to illustration, your work has set the stage for *Aria*. A very special thank you to NaBeela Washington for granting me the opportunity to work on this issue and whose brilliant, encouraging heart and fervent belief in this vision fueled my own passion for *Aria*. Lastly, thank you, reader, for being a curious spectator of *Aria* and watching the scenes unfold before you.

Sit back, read on, and enjoy the show!

ABIGAIL LOPEZ
GUEST EDITOR

ISBN 978-1-956076-97-4

GUEST EDITING by Abigail Lopez
ISSUE DESIGN by NaBeela Washington
ISSUE LAYOUT by Katreana Bellew
COVER ART by Grace Heinz and Caitlyn Lee
ISSUE INSPIRED by Ninel Nekay

Grace Angelica Heinz is an illustrator from Los Angeles who specializes in painting sweet-looking characters with a creepy twist.

Caitlyn Lee is currently a senior at Minneapolis College of Art and Design. Her works include narrative illustrations and comics.

Ninel Nekay is a Jamaican-American southerner, writer, actress, and Black mental health advocate. She has performed at some of the country's most historically groundbreaking venues such as The Fox Theatre, The John F. Kennedy Center for the Performing Arts, The National Center for Civil and Human Rights, and more.

Publication of *Lucky Jefferson* is made possible through community support.

Donate or submit to *Lucky Jefferson* on our website: luckyjefferson.com.

CAST

NINEL NEKAY

ALEJANDRA MEDINA

ASHLEY BAUMGARTNER

BOLU ADENIRAN

CATIE WILEY

CORI DIAZ

DONALD LOFTUS

HYBA OUAZZANI

KAT AGUDO

KATHARINE ARMBRESTER

KERRY TRAUTMAN

PETER DAKUTIS

ACT I

THE SHORTEST FILM

FADE IN:

INT. KITCHEN - AFTER MIDNIGHT

      HIM
      Do you love me?

      HER
      Yes, but when are you leaving?

HIM slams the door so viciously dinner plates backflip off the shelves.
HER collects the cracked ceramic & does not cut her feet on feelings that require
therapy.

FADE OUT:

NINEL NEKAY

EXT. FRONT LAWN

HIM stumbles outside, missing a step from the porch and his keys fall to the ground like silver compasses, buried directions in the dark.
HER opens the front door and follows him, hands bleeding from the ceramic shards.

>   HER
>   Don't drive tonight, just leave tomorrow!

>   HIM
>   Where the hell are my keys?

HER finds the keys and hides them behind her, and pockets them.
HIM hears the jingling and turns toward her like a rabid dog. HIM barks at her.

>   HER
>   Down!

HIM whimpers on the ground and exposes his belly beneath the blue button up shirt.
HER takes the keys out and shakes them in the air.
The jingle makes HIM roll over.

>   HIM
>   Give them to me, NOW.

>   HER
>   Not until you calm down.

HER locks the car with a loud double beep.

> HIM
> How *much* do you love me?

> HER
> Enough to give you a few more hours in my house.

> HIM
> *Our* house.

HER shakes her head and puts the keys in her pocket before HIM watches her go back inside the house again- *their* house.
A house he helped build.

FADE OUT:

KAT AGUDO

FADE IN:

INT. LIVING ROOM - MOMENTS LATER

HIM sits on the couch and stares blankly at a wall.
HER sits down next to him. They don't look at each other.

>HIM
>(quiet)
>I never said I was leaving.

>HER
>You didn't have to say it. I knew.

>HIM
>I wanted to love you. I really did.

HER nods silently as if speaking would make her cry.

>HIM (CONT'D)
>I'll pay you back for all those dishes. Blank check okay? You never believed in Venmo.

>HER
>Blank check is fine.

A beat.

>HIM
>Please say something.

>HER
>There's nothing to say.

HIM rests his hand on HER's. HER pulls her hand away.

> HIM
> (desperate)
> Please. Anything.

> HER
> Fine. Your breath smells like onions. You drink too much beer. I loved you so, so much.

> HIM
> I'm sorry...

HER stands up and crosses her arms.

> HER
> Now get out of my house.

FADE OUT:

CATIE WILEY

INT. AND EXT. BEDROOM – 30 MIN LATER

HER sits on the floor, against the bed.
HIM sits outside on a lawn chair, near the open window.

> HIM
> I know you're in there.

> HER
> Where else?

> HIM
> Anywhere.

> HER
> Where I want to be is here.

> HIM
> Me too.

> HER
> Tough shit.

> HIM
> I left. Like you asked.

> HER
> You're right there.

(cont.)

HIM slips off the chair, crawls toward the house, places his palms on the wall below the window.

> HIM
> You know how you leave a finished jigsaw puzzle on the table a few days, then realize it's been long enough, so you...hesitate then you crumple the Grecian ocean village or snowy forest or puppies in teacups or whatever between your hands, bust it up, sweep it over the edge into the box—

> HER
> And we're that obliterated puzzle?

> HIM
> All we have to do is put it back together—even glue it, frame it on the wall where it can't be broken.

> HER
> No.

HER stands, sits on the edge of bed.

> No we're more like...an opera. Our diva heaved that highest note to the balcony, shattered the crystal wine glass. There just isn't glue for that.

INT. KITCHEN - THE NEXT MORNING

HER is making breakfast, her movements are tense as if she's bracing for an upcoming fight. HIM enters, he slams the door just as harshly as last time.

>   HER
>   You came back?

>   HIM
>   Yes, you said you loved me.

>   HER
>   And I asked you to leave.

>   HIM
>   Because I scared you.

>   HER
>   You break things when you're angry.

>   HIM
>   I don't mean to…

>   HER
>   Even so.

HIM & HER take seats across from each other at the dining table.

HER places her plate in front of her and begins picking at her food. She's suddenly lost her appetite.

                                                        FADE OUT:

EXT. WEDDING RECEPTION – LATE AFTERNOON

>HER
>Congratulations.

>HIM
>You didn't have to come.

>HER
>(*Crushing decorative flowers in her hands*)
>I didn't?

>HIM
>(*Nervously*)
>She doesn't even know...

>HER
>I won't tell her.

>HIM
>(*Fiddling with his ring*)
>I wish you would.

>HER
>I don't have to.

HER leaves torn petals in her wake, traces of her already dissipating in the cold winter air.
HIM does not consider following when everything he's ever wanted is finally his. Almost everything.

FADE OUT:

INT. APARTMENT BUILDING LOBBY – AROUND MIDNIGHT

> HER
> (*Frustrated*)
> You can't keep coming here.

> HIM
> (*Leaning back against the wall, legs stretched out before him*)
> You're ignoring me.

> HER
> No. I'm moving on from you.

> HIM
> Don't. I haven't.

> HER
> (*Irritated*)
> Get up.

> HIM
> (*Reaching out to her*)
> You love me.

> HER
> (*Stepping back*)
> Go home. Lie in the bed you've made. Because I'm not going to.

HER steps into the elevator & stares at the floor until the doors close.
HIM watches the lights as she rises out of reach, leaving him behind.

ACT II

EXT. FRONT PORCH – AFTER MIDNIGHT

HIM darts back and forth like a bird encaged.
HER slides the kitchen window closed, shutting HIM out.

> HIM
> (at the window)
> Just say you love me and I'll go!

The lights go out within the house. HIM leaves.
After a moment, HER opens the door, three little words dangling from her lips.
They're carried away by the wind, unheard.

FADE OUT:

ALEJANDRA MEDINA

INT. KITCHEN – AFTERNOON

HER
I'm here.

HIM
'bout time. What's that?

HER
Isn't it stunning?

HIM
What the heck is it?

HER
It's a mask, silly. It's from South Africa, and it's—

HIM
You actually spent money on this?

HER
Of course! I didn't just walk out with it, like that time you walked out of Krispy Kremes without paying! You really don't like it?

HIM
It's not my thing.

HER
You have no culture.

HIM
If *that's* culture, I'm glad I haven't caught it.

HER
You have no appreciation for the finer things!

HIM
Yeah I do. Krispy Kremes. Now don't put that where I'll see it before I turn in. It'll give me nightmares.

HER
Why do you never like it when I bring home something different?
Foreign?

HIM
What's wrong with good old American art?

HER
I like variety, creativity…

HIM
Speaking of creative…what's for dinner?

HER
You are so…I'm afraid you are—

HIM
What?

HER
Never mind, just never mind.

HIM
Every time you come home with weird art we get into this same fight.

HER
And every time I'm afraid of finishing it. I got lamb chops for dinner.

FADE OUT:

KATHARINE ARMBRESTER

FADE IN:

INT. KITCHEN-THE NEXT DAY

> HIM
> Thank you for making dinner.

> HER
> My pleasure. I made it extra special...just for you.

> HIM takes a bite, gasps and falls to the floor.

FADE OUT:

DONALD LOFTUS

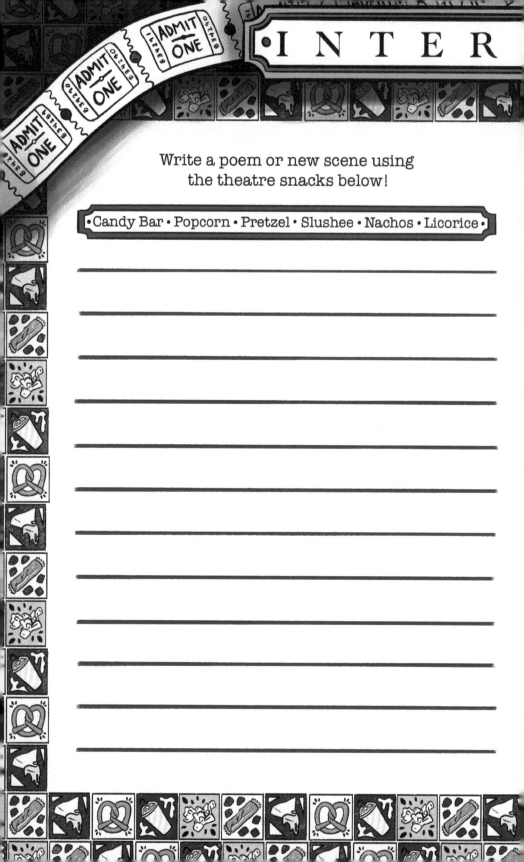

Write a poem or new scene using
the theatre snacks below!

•Candy Bar • Popcorn • Pretzel • Slushee • Nachos • Licorice•

Draw some of your favorite theatre snacks!

ACT III

INT. AQUARIUM – AFTERNOON

> HIM
> Can you forgive me?

> HER
> Grace is the thing with gills.

> HIM
> Thank you. I am awash in your purgation. I'll try to do better.

> HER
> (Pointing)
> Grace is the name of that banded butterflyfish.

HIM stomps off, but the storm is not that sore.

> HER
> Grace and I are not abashed.

HER listens as Grace sings a tune without words.

FADE OUT:

PETER DAKUTIS

INT. CHAPEL- MIDDAY

HIM is frantic. He paces back and forth in the middle of the aisle.

> HIM
> I still don't get it.

HER now sitting next to the podium.

> HER
> I've already explained why, at least fifty times.

> HIM
> And it still made zero sense.

> HER
> I'm so tired of explaining myself to someone that doesn't listen to understand.

> HIM
> Relax, I heard you. It's just not clicking.

> HER
> That's cause you don't want it to. You're blocking out what you don't want to hear.

> HIM
> Okay from the top one more time, this time slower.

> HER
> (deep sigh)
> I made a mistake by summoning you here. The consequences of my actions are right in front of me. It's consuming you. I need to make it stop before you get swallowed up.

> HIM
> And when did you decide on this?

HER
When you decided to destroy my kitchen last night.

HIM
That was an accident.

HER
So my bedframe, T.V, dining tables, chairs, my walls, oh and my car were accidents too?

HIM charges towards HER. HER rises.

HIM
You caused all of it!

HER stands her ground.

They're still for a minute, chests rising and falling.
The distance between them shrunken by the growing tension that's been brewing for weeks. HIM backs off, realizing that sudden impulse as a symptom.

HIM
I didn't choose to come back. You made that decision for me, against my will. Now it's only fair that I choose when or if I want to go back.

HER
Look at you. You're losing yourself. You'll never go back if it's up to you or it'll be too late. I knew the kind of person you were. The old you would let me fix this.

HIM
You decided you loved me too much to let me go. You brought me back. Now I love you too much to leave.

HER
I'm sorry.

HIM
Why?

HER
I killed you and I couldn't live with that. The truth is—I didn't love you, I just felt bad for you.

HIM
You don't mean that. We're soulmates.

HER
We never were. Your soul doesn't belong here anymore.

HIM approaches HER again. HIM gently pulls HER into his arms. HER accepts.

HIM
Please.

They settle into their desperate hug, so tight that if either of them pulled apart, they'd unravel.

BOLU ADENIRAN

End of play.

BONUS SCENE

INT. KITCHEN - AFTER MIDNIGHT

    HIM
    Do you love me?

    HER
    Yes, but when are you leaving?

HIM slams the door so viciously, dinner plates backflip off the shelves.

HER collects the cracked ceramic & does not cut her feet on feelings that require therapy.

    HER
    I said yes, didn't I? Don't slam the front door like that. If you break all the China in my parent's house, I'll never hear the end of it.

    HIM
    Why are you being so calm about this? You lost the match in front of everyone. You threw it for me, and for what? Because you love me?

    HER
    I didn't throw shit.

    HIM
    Oh, come on. We've been playing tennis together all summer at the leisure club and not once did I win against you. You're undefeated. Now we get to the summer match and what, you forgot how to play?

HIM sets the tennis racket bag on his shoulder onto the ground, letting it lean against the kitchen island. HER still hasn't looked at him.

    HER
    I guess you got lucky.

    HIM
    I guess you got fucking dense. I was only playing that match for fun. You were playing for the approval of your psychotic parents.

HER
You were playing to impress Coach Cooper. Now he knows you can defeat the undefeated. Won't that be great in the spring, when he goes back to coaching you at college?

HER carefully throws the cracked ceramic into a nearby trash can. HIM leans one hand onto the kitchen island in front of him, and uses the other hand to pinch the bridge of the nose.

HER
You didn't answer my question.

HIM
What question?

HER
When are you leaving?

HIM
Saturday.

HER
Oh. This weekend.

HIM
Yeah.

HER
I didn't realise it was so soon.

HIM
I tried not to think about it.

HER
That's a bit selfish, don't you think?

HIM
Selfish to avoid thinking about how much I don't want to leave you?

HER

I mean, you're the one leaving. You get to go back to college, surrounded by all your friends and all your potential. I'm the one who has to stay here. No plans. No hope.

HIM

You act like this is prison. I thought you loved living in East Hampton. You've been practically selling this place to me since I got here.

HER

It's not the place. There's just nothing here for me; especially when you leave.

HIM

Don't do that.

HER

I'm sorry. I'm sorry. It's just, you said so yourself - you'd go crazy if you were me. I do the same thing every day and have to sneak around my parents like a common criminal. What kind of life is that?

HIM

You're not glued to the ground. You can leave. Get out of here, and go far away from your parents.

HER

And do what? And go where?

HIM

You can figure it out. I know you can.

HER says nothing.

HIM

You're choosing complacency!

This strikes a chord with HER.

HER

Oh, I'm choosing it, huh? I wouldn't expect you to know a single thing about family obligation with the way you're granted all the freedom in the world.

HIM
Who the hell are you obligated to?

HER
My family's not like yours, okay? I can't just leave. To them, that's betrayal. To them, I'm turning my back on the people who gave me everything.

HIM
You're twenty-one! Do they expect you to live with them until you die?

HER
I don't need your holier-than-thou attitude right now. You're leaving, okay? You're leaving and we're never going to see each other again. What does it matter to you if I rot here when soon I'm just going to be a memory?

Looking for something to do with her hands, HER starts to rearrange the remaining plates on the shelves so that it doesn't look as obviously empty. HIM is using his hands to speak; to convey emotion.

HIM
Do you think I don't care about what happens to you? I love you. You know that.

HER
You clearly don't love me enough to stay.

HIM
Is that what you want? For us to die here together? What, we'll play tennis in the mornings and drink at night? What will we do when it's chilly? Switch to table tennis?

HER
If you loved me, then it wouldn't matter what we did.

HIM
And there you go again! You live in a fantasy world. I need a degree, and a career. Good for you for being rich enough to not need college, but some of us don't get a fighting chance.

HER
You know what? You are selfish. You're selfish for ever making me fall for you. You're selfish for kissing me in the first place.

HIM
That's not fair, and you know that. Feelings are nonsensical.

HER
No, we're nonsensical. We never should have -

HIM
Do you really want to play the game of 'should have' and 'shouldn't have?'

HER
No. I want to play the game of you getting out of my house, and me coming up with a way to explain to my mother why her favourite salad bowl is broken.

HIM
So, you're just going to kick me out like that. You want to spend our last few days before I leave mad at each other? How did you love me enough to risk your reputation by purposely losing the tennis game, but not enough to let me go back to school without this weight on my back?

HER
That's me loving myself enough to be honest with you. Sorry you didn't like it. Take your cheap racket off my floor and leave.

HIM does as instructed and takes his racket bag off the ground. He opens the front door again, but HER speaking stops HIM.

HER
Wait.

HIM turns to HER, expectant.

Please stay.

HER
(vulnerable)

HIM shakes his head in disbelief. He laughs almost self-deprecatingly.

HIM
Now that's selfish.

He exits out the front door. When she's sure she's gone, HER picks up a plate and throws it to the front door. She falls to the ground with it.

THE LUCKYS

A.K.A "The Tonys"! Here's your chance to be a judge!
After reading the issue, write down your top picks
for the awards below:

BEST SCENE:

_____

MOST SHOCKING:

_____

MOST LAUGH OUT LOUD WORTHY:

_____

FAVORITE DIALOGUE:

_____

WHAT'S NEXT

Upcoming Calls For Submissions: *Gibberish*

Issue 9 explores the celebration of ethnic and strange names, their meanings, values, and beyond. Join us as we delve into foreign words that retain cultural and personal significance to the writer.

Poems, flash fiction, essays, hybrid forms, and art are all welcome.

Submissions Open: December 1, 2021

LUCKY JEFFERSON'S LITERARY ARTISTS

Josie O'Neal-Odom and CJ Han designed the alternate cover on page 1.

Based in NYC, Josie O'Neal-Odom is an illustration major at Parsons School of Design. Her work can be found on Instagram @pheenydoodles.

CJ Han is an Illustrator and Fine Artist from New Jersey. They have a strong passion for storytelling, whether it be through illustration, animation, or comic art.

Gabriela Vega designed the artwork on pages 38-39.

Gabriela Vega is a student at Cal State Fullerton pursuing her degree in Illustration. Her dream after graduating, is to work as a children's book illustrator.

FOLLOW US ONLINE

 @LUCKY_JEFFERSON

 @LUCKYJEFFERSONLIT

 @_LUCKYJEFFERSON

USE #ARIA, #THESHOWGOESON,
OR #LJSQUAD TO FOLLOW
THE CONVERSATION

+

TAKE A SELFIE
WITH YOUR COPY
OF ARIA AND TAG US!